Team Reader

MISSY

by Terence Blacker

Illustrated by Claudia Flor

Ernst Klett Sprachen
Stuttgart

Bookmark

The bookmark can help you with difficult words.

These words are marked with * in the text.

In case you lose the bookmark, you can download it.

Contents

Digital resources 2

Team Read 4

Characters 4

MY
CHAPTERS ✓

Chapter 1   Ⓜ Ⓙ Ⓣ .... 7 ☐

Chapter 2   Ⓜ Ⓙ Ⓣ .... 17 ☐

Chapter 3   Ⓜ .... 24 ☐

Chapter 4   　 Ⓙ .... 30 ☐

Chapter 5   　 　 Ⓣ .... 35 ☐

Chapter 6   Ⓜ .... 40 ☐

Chapter 7   　 　 Ⓣ .... 46 ☐

Chapter 8   　 Ⓙ .... 52 ☐

Chapter 9   Ⓜ Ⓙ Ⓣ .... 58 ☐

Chapter 10   Ⓜ Ⓙ Ⓣ .... 69 ☐

Chapter 11   　 　 Ⓣ .... 76 ☐

Chapter 12   　 Ⓙ .... 82 ☐

Chapter 13   Ⓜ .... 86 ☐

Chapter 14   Ⓜ Ⓙ Ⓣ .... 91 ☐

Chapter 15   Ⓜ Ⓙ Ⓣ .... 99 ☐

Chapter 16   Ⓜ Ⓙ Ⓣ .... 107 ☐

Team Read

Choose one of the following characters and tick the box. Read only your character's chapters and those chapters that *everybody* has to read.

Of course …

You *can* always read the whole story and discover everything that's going on at Barrow Hill School for yourself.

Read chapters for M:
1, 2, 3, 6, 9, 10, 13, 14, 15, 16

MARKO

Choose to follow Marko if you do not read books very often or if you feel that long texts in English are confusing. Find out what Marko has discovered in the Old Music Room – but be careful: *it's spooky …!*

Read chapters for **J**:
1, 2, 4, 8, 9, 10, 12, 14, 15, 16

JAMIE

Jamie is not only facing the mystery at school but he also has problems at home. If you sometimes read books or if you don't find English too difficult, read Jamie's chapters. Find out what trouble he's in. What *dangerous* plan will he come up with …?

Read chapters for **T**:
1, 2, 5, 7, 9, 10, 11, 14, 15, 16

TRI

Tri discovers what lies behind the Old Music Room mystery but suddenly she's faced with a tough decision: *her friends* or *her future*…? If you read a lot or if you like English and find it really easy, read Tri's chapters. What has she discovered about the mystery?

Chapter 1

JAMIE

Here is how the strangeness begins.

I'm walking across the school playground on my way to a small brick* building we call the Old Music Room. School is over for the day, and I have practice with my band Eye Trouble (or I Trouble, we keep changing the name).

Outside the Old Music Room, I stop, then listen.

A noise is coming from the building.

A thumping, shouting, screaming noise.

The Old Music Room is rocking. And not in a good way.

I look through the only window in the building. A small figure is moving around in there, thumping the tables with his hands, yelling* as he goes.

It's Marko, the bass player in the band, and he seems to be going mad.

MARKO

ME: *7^)$%8!

~#+*!&?$%%!

JAMIE

Marko is small, and a year younger than Tri and me. He has wild red hair and bright blue eyes. Normally he is very quiet, but not now.

Could he be practising a new song? I don't think so. Eye Trouble may not be great, but we are better than this.

I have a strong feeling inside that things are about to get weird.

I take a deep breath, and open the door.

MARKO

ME: '~#+*!&?$%%%! *%^?#@!

Aaaaarrrrgggghhhh! Aaaa-'

I am shouting.

I am screaming.

I might even be swearing*.

In the middle of shouting really loudly, I see Jamie. He is standing at the door.

Jamie is in the year above me. He's my friend, but sometimes he looks at me like he's some kind of teacher.

JAMIE: 'What's up, Marko?'

I spread my arms.

ME: 'Look! Look at all this! ~{+*$%!'

Jamie frowns*. He looks around the room. Now he sees why I'm angry.

There are books and sheets of music all over the floor.

The music stand is broken and is lying in one corner. A cup has been thrown at the piano.

There are sharp broken pieces of china* on the black and white keys*.

Chairs have been pushed over.

Jamie: *(in a sad voice)* 'Oh, Marko, what have you done?'

Everybody always blames* me. Even my so-called friends.

Me: *(angry)* 'It wasn't me. I found it like this. Someone has trashed* the room.'

Jamie: 'But why?'

Me: 'I don't know. @~{£^&%! ~{@&^£&*!'

JAMIE

A word about Marko.

He has what teachers call 'issues'*. Temper* issues. Learning issues. Fitting-in issues. Doing-what-he's-told issues. Think of an issue, and Marko's got it.

There's a rumour* at school that his mum and dad came here with a group of travellers (we're not supposed* to call them gypsies*) when Marko was about five. They moved on, but Marko was left behind. These days, his grandma looks after him.

No one has ever seen Marko's grandma. Sometimes I think she may not even exist.

One day in the playground, my friend Tri – the third member of our group – stopped some of the younger kids bullying him. After that, he started following her around and somehow he ended up coming to our music practice sessions. Tri lent him a bass ukulele that her parents gave her.

Big surprise: little Marko was good. When he plays the bass these days, his face changes. All the tension* and anger seem to be lifted* from it. He is calm, and sways* in time to the music. Sometimes you can almost see a smile on his lips.

Another thing about Marko. He doesn't say much, but when he does, he always tells the truth. He won't lie, even if it means he'll get into trouble *(which he always does)*.

And that is why right now, as I look around the trashed music room, I believe him – just as I have believed him before. Fact is, this isn't the first time the music room has been trashed…

I get down on my knees and start picking up the music books which have been thrown on the floor.

It's at this moment that the door opens and Tri walks in. She's humming a tune* and wanders over to the piano.

TRI

I think it's going to be a jazz thing. I can feel that. It will be the kind of song you might hear in an old-fashioned black-and-white movie. I sing a couple of lines out loud.

JAMIE: 'Tri…'

> *'The day*
> *May be grey,*
> *But hey,*
> *In this heart of mine*
> *It's summertime –'*

JAMIE: 'Tri…!'

> *'Skies of blue,*
> *Boo-boo-be-loo –*

'Ouch!' Something sharp pricks* my finger.

JAMIE: 'Tri!!'

I stop playing and notice for the first time that Jamie and Marko are standing there, staring at me.

'*Ouch* ... I cut my finger,' I cry, sucking the tip of my finger. 'I'm actually bleeding*.'

'What's going on?' I ask. They don't answer.

I notice that their eyes are on the door behind me.

I hear an adult, a man, coughing behind me.
I turn, and there, filling the frame of the doorway,
is none other than the large – OK, fat – figure of
our headteacher Mr Attiah.

He is looking around the room, and is not pleased
by what he sees. Now I look a bit closer myself,
the place does seem to be in a bit of a mess*.

'Katrina. James. Marko.' The headteacher speaks
quietly, which is always a sign of trouble.
'My office. All of you. Now. We need to talk.'

Chapter 2

JAMIE

We don't believe in leaders* in Eye Trouble because we like to think that we're all equal* but, if there were a leader, it would be Katrina Marybelle Elio, better known as Tri.

Tri is tall, black and really hot. She always has an answer when someone criticises her. She's an amazing musician and has the coolest parents on the planet *(her father is a saxophonist in a band and her mother has a fashion business)*.

At first, Marko and I thought it was a bit of a miracle that she wanted to hang out with us, but these days we've got used to the fact that – strange but true – she likes us, and she likes our music.

As we follow Mr Attiah across the playground, there is only one thought in my mind.

Leave this to Tri.

TRI

We follow the headteacher into the school building, up the stairs. He beckons us into his office. We stand in front of his big desk.

I've seen how my mother deals* with difficult situations, like the time I once accidentally* walked out of a music shop with a harmonica in my pocket. She puts on a big, wide smile and says…

MARKO

TRI: *(in a strong voice)* 'I think there's been a bit of a misunderstanding.'

Tri is good at words.

She says things that would take me two days to think* up.

TRI: 'We noticed that there was a bit of a mess in the music room when we arrived. We were just clearing it up.'

MR ATTIAH: 'And who was the first to arrive at the scene of the crime*?' He looks over his glasses – *at me*. 'Let me guess.'

I blush*. I can't help it. I always blush, even when I've done nothing wrong.

It has gone quiet in the room. I think I have to say something.

ME: 'It's like she said. It wasn't me who made the mess.'

MR ATTIAH: 'Someone was acting like a bull* in a china shop. Shouting and swearing. Who was that?'

ME: 'Me.'

MR ATTIAH: 'Hmmmm. Surprise, surprise.'

TRI

Everybody likes Mr Attiah. We all know that he's fair. He doesn't allow bullying by the older children. He laughs at jokes, which I think is quite unusual in a headteacher.

But he does like a cliché. If he can find a phrase or saying that has been used about a billion times too often, even if it has nothing to do with what he is saying, he'll use it.

Sometimes, when he is teaching our class history, I count the number of clichés he uses in one lesson.

My record is 53.

JAMIE

'Let's not count our chickens before they're hatched*,' says Mr Attiah.

We're all thinking, *What*?

And this is where we get our first surprise.

'Which one of you is the computer nerd*?'
Mr Attiah asks.

We look at one another, confused.

'Hah! Silence is golden, eh?' The headteacher sighs*. 'Yesterday afternoon, the Sixth Form choir was in the Old Music Room. One of the girls left her mobile phone behind. When she collected it this morning, she found that the memory had been wiped*. As clean as a whistle.'

Tri breathes in and seems to grow by about six inches.

'I'm sorry, Mr Attiah, but we know nothing about any of this,' she says in her *I-know-my-rights* voice. 'We were tidying the room up. We never even saw a phone.'

'Yes, yes.' The headteacher waves a hand as if he's wiping a blackboard.

Then he reaches for something on his desk, and holds it up, as if it's another piece of evidence*.

TRI

This is where it gets really strange.

In Mr Attiah's hand is one of the old music books which gather* dust* on the shelf in the Old Music Room.

'A book of old Victorian songs has been defaced*, as you can see.' He points to the front of the book. 'Time and again, that room has been left topsy-turvy. I cannot turn a blind eye to it. I am locking* up the Old Music Room as from today. It will be demolished* next year to make room for a new storeroom*.'

'But what about our –?'

The headteacher ignores me. 'You three are out of control. I gave you an inch and you took a mile,' he says. 'I shall be writing about your behaviour to your parents and –' he glances* at Marko –'your grandparent.'

MARKO

But now we're not listening.

Our eyes are on the music book.

JAMIE:

Scrawled across the front of the book are five letters, written untidily in blood-red ink*.

TRI

One word. One mysterious word.

'MISSY'.

Chapter 3

MARKO

I always feel alone.

I was alone on the day I woke up in my nan's* house and I knew that my mum and dad had gone forever.

I am alone in the playground when the children call* me names.

I am alone in lessons when our teacher Miss Gordon asks me a question and sighs when I don't know the answer.

And I am alone that day when Mr Attiah looks at me and says, 'Surprise, surprise'.

I always feel alone. That's just the way it is.

After we leave the headteacher's room, Tri puts a hand on my shoulder.

TRI: 'Don't worry, Marko. We'll sort* this out. Will you be in trouble with your nan?'

ME: 'I don't think so.'

My nan is not the worrying kind.

That evening, when I get home, she is watching TV.

As usual.

She doesn't hear me come into the flat.

As usual.

A bottle of red wine is on the table beside her.

As usual.

She sometimes says the bottle is her only real friend because it never lets* her down.

ME: 'Hi, Nan. I'm home.'

NAN: 'Hullo, love. Did you have a good day?'

ME: 'Not really.'

NAN: 'Great. That's good, love.'

ME: 'I'm going out later, Nan.'

NAN: 'Yeah?'

I go to the kitchen and make myself some toast.

Later, after it gets dark, I notice Nan has gone to sleep. There's a cigarette smoking in the ash-tray beside her. I pinch the end. She gets annoyed* when she wakes up and the cigarette has burned itself out.

Then I leave the flat.

I go down the stone stairs and on to the street.

I walk to school, thinking, thinking.

Someone is trashing our music room and it's happening at night. I want to find out who it is that's doing it.

I climb the wire* fence into the playground. I'm a good climber. Sometimes I come here in the evenings.

I like the school playground, especially when no one else is here.

I walk towards the music room.

I'm as quiet as a weasel.

Then I stop.

Am I dreaming?

There are no lights in the building, but I can hear music.

Piano music.

Someone is playing the piano in the dark.

I creep* forward. I crouch below the window.
My heart is thumping.

Slowly, slowly I stand until my eyes are above the
windowsill*.

At first, I see nothing in the blackness of the
room.

Then, against the white of the piano keys, I can
see something move.

There is a shadow on the piano stool. It's swaying
backwards and forwards.

Now my eyes begin to see something in the
darkness.

A small woman in a long black dress is sitting in
front of the piano.

She has long, dark curly* hair. It's like a black cloud
around her head.

As I watch, the music stops.

The woman's hands slip* from the piano.

She turns slowly.

She has a small, pale* face.

She stares at me…

– and smiles.

I run.

Chapter 4

JAMIE

I'm in my room when my parents come home with my little sister Lisbeth. I hear the key in the front door lock and suddenly the house is full of the sounds of a happy family.

'What a *clever* girl you are,' my mother is saying.

'*Well done*, Lisbeth,' says my dad.

My sister is four years old, and my parents think that she is the genius the world has been waiting for.

'James!' my mother calls.

I stand at the top of the stairs. 'What's she done this time?' I speak in a sarcastic voice. 'Written a symphony? Found a cure* for cancer?'

'Good evening, James.' Dad flashes a fake* smile in my direction. In a quieter voice, he says to Mum, 'I'll get Lisbeth her tea.'

Uh-oh. When my father does his vanishing* act, it's never a good sign. It means that one of my mother's talks is on the way.

'We've had an email from Mr Attiah.' She looks up the stairs and the temperature in the hall drops about 50 degrees. 'He told me what you and others did to the music room.'

'Others?'

'Your… *friends*.' As she says the word 'friends', she looks as if she has just smelt something very nasty*.

I sit down on the top stair. 'Which friends are those, Mum? I've got *loads* of friends.'

'You know that's not true, James. We often worry about how few friends you have.'

'Thanks, Mum.'

'I'm talking about the tall black girl with the loud voice and the little traveller kid.'

'They *have* got names, you know.'

'I'm sure Katrina and Marko are very nice in their own way. It's just that *their* way is *a little* different from ours.'

'I happen to like them.'

My mother opens her arms to me. 'Come here, Jamie.'

I walk slowly down the stairs, then stand in front of her. She puts hers arms around me. I lean* away from her.

'We love you very much,' she says softly into my right ear. 'We just want the best for you. We hate to see you unhappy. The problem's your school, isn't it?'

'No.' I say the words into her hair.

'Of course it is. Barrow Hill School is fine for a certain type of child. It's great that it's so … mixed.'

She holds me closer as if to stop me talking.

'But maybe it's a bit *too* mixed for you. It's holding you back, isn't it? We want the best for you. That's why we've decided to move you to St Matthews School next term*. You'll be with children who are more your type. It's a wonderful school. They get fantastic results.'

I push away from her. 'I don't want to.'

'It's decided,' she says. 'This business with the music room has made up our minds for us.'

'But we didn't do anything wrong.'

My mother holds up her hand and smiles like a vicar* in church. 'It's all forgotten,' she says.

'There's nothing to forget!'

The smile vanishes. 'We're your parents, James.' My mother's voice is ice-cold. 'We want the very best for you. We are not prepared to stand by and watch you fail*.'

'Fail? Am I failing?'

'You know perfectly well what I mean.'

'But I –'

'Good.' She walks towards the kitchen.

Conversation over.

Chapter 5

TRI

Sometimes I can be a little obsessive*. As soon as something gets into my brain*, it takes over. I can't think of anything else.

It might be a few notes of music that are trying to become a song. Or a question that I can't answer in class. Or sometimes just a word.

Like 'Missy'.

Who is Missy? *What* is Missy?

The day after our visit to Mr Attiah's office, I see Jamie while we are waiting for our teacher Miss Phelps to arrive for our first lesson. I ask him what he thinks about the Missy thing.

He just shrugs* and stares at his desk. I like Jamie, but he can be very moody sometimes.

I catch up with Marko during morning break. He never talks much and today, when I mention our little chat with Mr Attiah, he doesn't even seem to be listening. As I talk, he stares at me with those wide blue eyes. It almost seems as if he wants to tell me something.

That's how we are, the three of us. Sometimes we tell each other stuff. Other times we keep quiet. Each of us likes to go our own way.

Meanwhile, I'm still thinking about Missy. Who would write that word on an old music book? And why?

At the end of the school day, I wander over towards the Old Music Room. It's locked.

My parents won't be home yet and so I decide to go to the school library to do my homework.

The library is empty.

I sit at a corner table in the History section of the library and absent-mindedly* glance at the shelves.

I notice a small, dark green book, so thin that it might almost be a magazine or a pamphlet, wedged between two large history books. For some reason, I reach for it to look more closely. It's very old and, judging* by the way the binding* cracks* as I open it, it has not been read for years.

Its title is *The Annual Register of Barrow Hill School, 1882-3.*

I'm leafing* through its pages when a piece of paper falls out. It's brown and faded*, as if it has been cut out of a very old magazine. In one corner, there is some handwriting that has turned pale* yellow over the years. I can only just read the words 'Pall Mall Gazette, September 1882'.

The headline* makes me gasp*. I begin to read.

THREE CHILDREN SAVED FROM A SCHOOL FIRE

A n event occurred* last Tuesday evening, September 3rd, which we shall find difficult to describe in mere words. We must therefore refer* readers to our illustration which pictures the tragic scene.

At Barrow Hill School in south London, a music room, in which three young pupils were being taught by Miss Dorothea Bryant, a music teacher, was found to be ablaze* by people passing on the street nearby.

Courageously, they entered the inferno and rescued the terrified children. Alas, we must report that the teacher was later reported to have died in the catastrophe.

Shocking as it will seem to our readers, it appears* that the fire was started by the victim* herself. Miss Bryant, who was sometimes known to the children as "Missy", had been dismissed* from her position the day before because God-fearing parents had complained* about her bad influence on their children.

THREE CHILDREN SAVED FROM A SCHOOL FIRE

I look through the list of teachers' names in the register. There is no mention of Miss Dorothea Bryant.

Missy had been rubbed* out of history.

Chapter 6

MARKO

People think I'm strange because I don't talk very much.

In my life, I have learned that it is sometimes better to keep quiet. Saying things can get you into trouble.

I don't trust words.

At school I want to tell Tri what I saw last night, but I'm worried that she'll also think I'm strange. If people find out that I sometimes climb into the school playground after dark, I could be sent to see Mr Attiah again.

Tri: 'Are you all right, Marko? You look really pale.'

Me: 'I'm fine.'

Tri: 'I've got a new song. We'll have to find somewhere else to practise now that the music room is locked.'

Me: 'OK.'

At lunchtime I go to the Old Music Room. Tri is right. The door is locked.

All afternoon I worry about this. If the building is locked, how did the dark-haired lady get in?

Maybe I dreamed the whole thing.

I need to find out.

A long time ago my dad showed me something he called 'the magic key'. It was a piece of wire which he had bent* in a special way. He showed me how it could open any door.

The only thing I have that reminds* me of him is the magic key. I keep it in the drawer* beside my bed.

That night, after I've had some toast and Nan's fallen asleep in front of the television, I leave the flat with the magic key in my pocket.

I go to school. The moon is bright in the sky. I climb the fence. I cross the playground.

She is there. As I walk towards the Old Music Room, I hear the tune I heard last night. Its notes softly float through the night air.

I creep up to the window. I see the shadow swaying backwards and forwards as she plays the piano. She begins to sing.

Her voice is gentle*. She sounds like a mum singing her child to sleep.

There is nothing frightening* about that voice. I feel braver now.

I reach for the magic key in my back pocket and walk to the door.

It's easy. The lock opens after a few seconds. My father would be proud of me.

Slowly, I open the door.

The dark-haired lady keeps playing. The moonlight shines through the window, lighting the room.

I can see her small fingers press gently on the keys.

Her black dress.

Her dark curly hair like a shadowy cloud around her head.

Her pale face, with cheeks* that seem to sparkle* in the light.

Tears! The dark-haired lady is crying.

The song she sings is the saddest thing I've ever heard.

THE DARK-HAIRED LADY:

> *'Every night when the sun goes down,*
>
> *Every night when the sun goes down,*
>
> *Every night when the sun goes down,*
>
> *I hang my head and cry.'*

I slowly walk across the room.

Soon I am looking at her over the piano.

THE DARK-HAIRED LADY:

> *'I wish every day I could go home,*
>
> *I wish every day I could go home...'*

ME: *(quietly)* 'How did you get in?'

Her head down, she keeps playing.

ME: 'Excuse me, Miss, but how did you get in here? Do you have a key?'

THE DARK-HAIRED LADY:

'I hang my head and cry.'

Her song comes to an end. She sighs, lowers her hands and raises* her head so that she is staring me in the face, her eyes sparkling with tears.

No one has ever looked at me like that. She is looking right into me.

She can see my loneliness.

And how I miss my mum.

She understands.

ME: 'I was wondering, Miss. Who are you?'

She smiles.

Just a normal, nice, friendly smile.

And then she speaks: 'Hullo, Marko.'

Chapter 7

TRI

Someone is playing games. That's my first thought. Some joker has read the story of the fire and has decided to play a silly pretend-ghost trick on us.

But who would know that there had been a fire?

And that a music teacher had died in it?

And that her nickname was 'Missy'?

Another possibility occurs* to me. It's not a silly pretend-ghost trick at all. It's real. Missy is back.

Usually I can talk to Jamie about this sort* of thing, but two days after our meeting with the headteacher, he is still acting like someone with the troubles of the world on his shoulders. I'm guessing that now is not the time to discuss whether we are being stalked* by the ghost of a psycho Victorian music teacher.

Instead, I decide that I'll ask to see Mr Attiah. I want to tell him that it's wrong that we have been banned from the Old Music Room for something we haven't done. We need to practise. Call me crazy, but I honestly believe at that moment that I can get him to take me seriously.

Wrong.

When I enter the headteacher's office, I'm surprised to see he's not alone. On a chair beside his desk is the grey-haired figure of my class teacher Miss Phelps. She's sitting up so straight that she reminds* me of a phrase my mum sometimes likes to use.

She is 'as relaxed as a coiled* spring'.

Mr Attiah stands up as I walk in. 'Ah, Katrina. Take a seat.' He waves a hand at the seat in front of his desk. 'I thought it would be useful if Miss Phelps were here. A problem aired* is a problem shared. We can discuss your general situation.'

My *general situation*? I don't like the sound of this at all.

'I just wanted to talk about the music room,' I say in my most reasonable* voice.

Mr Attiah holds up a hand. 'Let's kill two birds with one stone. Miss Phelps has an excellent plan.'

A big, phony smile appears* on my class teacher's face. She turns slowly towards Mr Attiah.

'Katrina is a great asset* to the class, sir. Bright, full of ideas, a talented musician. And that is why I think that she should join our Music Conservatory programme.

What?

'Ah, good idea.' Mr Attiah frowns thoughtfully, as if this were some big surprise.

Miss Phelps turns to me.

'Katrina, you may not know about this programme because it's usually open only to pupils in the Sixth and Lower Sixth forms. The Music Conservatory, which is a short bus ride from here, takes three pupils from Barrow Hill for special tuition*. You would be playing with top musicians. It will be a marvellous opportunity* for you.'

'Excellent idea. If you can't beat them, join them.'
Mr Attiah brings his hands together in a sort of
silent clap. 'What do you think of that, Katrina?'

'What about the Old Music Room?' I ask. 'Could
we still use it for practising with Jamie and
Marko?'

Mr Attiah winces*. 'Katrina, now is not the time to
look a gift* horse in the mouth. You'd be heading
for the top, going for gold.'

I must be looking uncertain*, because he leans*
forward on his desk.

'Time heals, Katrina.' His voice is as smooth as
honey. 'A friend in need is a friend indeed*, but
sometimes you can be held back by your friends.
Marko is a very –' He frowns as he looks for the
right word – 'special boy. And the other one, er –'

'James,' says Miss Phelps.

'Yes, of course, James. I'm sure James has his
talents, too. But are they high-flyers? Are they
a cut above the rest? I don't think so. This move
will be good for you, your parents and even our
school. It's a no-brainer*.'

'Can I think about it, Mr Attiah?'

Miss Phelps starts* in her seat as if someone has pricked her with a pin*.

'Think about it, Katrina?' cries Miss Phelps, sounding like an angry chicken. 'I thought you were ambitious*.'

Mr Attiah sighs. 'Of course. Discuss it with your parents.'

I stand up and am just about to leave when I remember the reason for my visit. 'I was in the library yesterday. I read about the fire which destroyed the first music room.'

Mr Attiah has reached for a letter on his desk and is pretending to read it. 'Time waits for no man,' he mutters.

'A teacher died in that fire,' I say. 'Her nickname was Missy.'

The headteacher looks up sharply.

'Yes,' I say. 'And that was the name on the music book.'

Mr Attiah puts down the letter and smooths it out with both hands. 'We have just offered you a big chance –'

'But –'

'Opportunity knocks, young lady. Give it your best* shot.'

Chapter 8

JAMIE

Suddenly there is a wall around me. Or maybe the wall has always been there but I have never noticed it before.

After my parents have told me that they were taking me away from Barrow Hill School, I hide behind my wall. I am silent in class. Whenever mum or dad talk to me, I answer with a shrug*.

Tri tells me she has some news – I give her a cold look and walk away. I notice that Marko stays close to me at break and I know that he wants to talk to me, but I ignore him.

I hear my mother's words.

We are not going to stand by and let you fail.

And that is the reason I am being taken from school.

I am a failure*.

Behind my wall, I am safe. I'm alone and it's better that way.

At the end of school on the second day of my great silence, Tri tells me that she's going to see Mr Attiah about the music room. She asks me to wait for her so that we can walk home together.

I nod my agreement but, as soon as she has left, I am out of the school gate.

I walk and walk. On the main road, I go into a shop. While the old lady behind the counter* is getting my change* from the till*, I slip* a bar of chocolate into my pocket.

I have never stolen anything before, but now it seems just fine. Nothing matters. Stealing is what failures do.

Leaving the shop, I wander the streets, taking as long as I can to get home. I have put up the hood* of my coat so that people can't see my face. Sometimes, as adults walk past me, I notice that they give me a suspicious* look as if I am some kind of problem. My wall has turned me into a scary person. To tell the truth, I quite like it.

Eventually I reach a bus station. I find a bench*, sit down and take out my (stolen) bar of chocolate. I eat it slowly. It's probably the most delicious bar of chocolate I have ever tasted.

What if I just got on a bus? I could stay on it until, in the dark of the evening, it reached wherever it was going.

I look at the names of towns on the front of each bus and wonder what life would be like if I just moved there tonight. Bromley, Croydon, Dartford, Penge.

After a while, I notice that it is almost dark. I must have been on my bench, dreaming, for quite a while. People are coming home from work. As they walk past me, some of them look at me with a hurried, unfriendly look. It's time to move.

I slowly walk home, but when I reach the street where I live, I find that I don't want to go inside yet. I don't belong there.

There's a park opposite my house. I walk through its gates, climb over a little fence and sit under a big tree. From where I am sitting, I can see into our kitchen. I watch my family coldly, as if I were a stranger.

Moments later, my mother walks into the kitchen and puts something on the cooker. She turns on the radio and is singing to herself as she watches the pot*. Then my dad is there, carrying Lisbeth. As they talk, he puts my sister on a chair at the kitchen table.

They look happy. They are better without me, and my *failure*.

When I walk into the house, I'll spoil* that perfect family scene.

The evening air is getting colder now and the damp* is seeping* through my trousers.

I stand up. For a reason I don't understand, I feel stronger now.

As I finally make my way out of the bushes to go home, I notice something on the ground. It's an empty box of matches*.

I pick it up and hold it in my hand.

It's at that moment that I have my big, brilliant, dangerous idea.

Chapter 9

MARKO

I don't like secrets. They make me feel bad inside.

Sometimes I tell them to nan* as she watches TV.

When I finish, she drinks some wine and says nothing.

ME: 'And so that's my big secret, Nan.'

NAN: 'Oh yeah? What's on the other channel, love?'

It's like dropping the secret down a well*.

But now I have a secret which I have to tell Tri and Jamie.

It's about what I have seen.

They don't believe me.

I text them and ask them to meet me at the Old Music Room.

At first they don't like the idea.

They agree.

Tonight they'll meet the dark-haired lady.

JAMIE

It's dark, cold and past eight o'clock when I arrive at the school gates. I told my parents I had music practice at Tri's house. They said I couldn't go. So, while they were putting Lisbeth to bed, I left.

Tri and Marko are at the school gates when I arrive. They both look so guilty that I almost laugh out loud.

'This had better be worth it,' Tri mutters.
'My parents will kill me if they find out.'

Marko gives her one of his scary, dead-eyed looks.

'Follow me,' he says.

TRI

And, before Jamie or I can say anything, he has gone.

But he is not walking anywhere, or even running. He's climbing.

Up the wire* fence he goes, as quick as a cat climbing a tree. The fence is about six feet* high

but, within seconds, he is looking at us through the wire on the other side.

I check no one is coming down the street, then I climb up. Swearing to himself, Jamie follows.

MARKO

We're in.

All three of us.

I walk across the playground.

When I get close to the Old Music Room, I stop to listen.

TRI: 'Marko, you've got to tell us –'

ME: 'Shh!'

We stand in silence. The only noise is the sound of traffic.

I reach into my back pocket.

JAMIE

Whoa. Now I'm impressed.

Marko has a bent* piece of wire in his hand. He walks to the door, puts the wire in the lock, fiddles with it for a moment. The door opens.

TRI

It takes a few moments for our eyes to get used to the darkness.

Marko stares at the piano for a moment. Then he walks to a corner on the far side of the room where there are some chairs. He sits down.

'We'll wait,' he whispers.

Jamie sits down beside him. He looks miserable again.

'Are you all right?' I ask.

He shrugs*.

'I might as well tell you now,' he says.

JAMIE

I'm glad it's dark. I can't see their faces as I tell them I'll be leaving school.

When I finish, Tri puts a hand on my arm.
'Oh, Jamie,' she says. 'I'm so sorry.'

'Stuff happens,' I say.

I glance across at Marko, expecting him to say something.

He is staring at the piano.

MARKO

She is here.

First I see the keys of the piano moving.

Then I see the beginnings of a shadow.

Gently, very quietly at first, music starts to play.

It's the tune she played yesterday.

Beside me, I hear a little gasp* of fear. Jamie and Tri have seen what is happening.

The tune ends.

We can see her more clearly now. She turns in her seat to face us.

There is a smile on her small, pale* face.

Dark-haired lady: 'Good evening, children.'

TRI AND JAMIE

Aaaaarrrrgggghhh!

JAMIE

Tri grabs me around the arm and squeezes so tightly* that it begins to hurt.

Marko stands. Then he actually begins to walk *towards* the thing at the piano.

'Hullo.' He speaks in a quiet voice, as if she is a wild animal he doesn't want to frighten*. 'These are my friends, Jamie and Tri.'

The dark figure stands up and takes two steps towards us.

And then – oh no, please no – it starts to speak.

TRI

'My name is Miss Bryant.' The voice is quiet, yet firm*. The accent is very precise, like someone out of an old film. 'I am your music teacher.'

Jamie manages* to speak. 'H-h-h-how do you do, Miss Bryant?' he croaks.

She laughs, an odd* sound like leaves* being blown gently across the ground.

'You can call me Missy,' she says.

MARKO

Tri seems less afraid now.

TRI: 'I've read about you. There was a fire.'

MISSY: *(smiling)* 'I saved the children. The naughty* things had knocked* over a lamp.'

TRI: 'And you got the blame.'

MISSY: 'I am your teacher. That is what matters. I shall be here at all times to help you with your music.'

JAMIE: 'Actually, there may be a bit of a problem there.'

JAMIE

I'm trying to be helpful. So I explain that the music room is now locked up because of the mess she made.

She seems to find that funny. 'Oh dear. I am a bit of a messy* one, aren't I?' she says.

'Also you wiped the memory of a mobile phone.'

She looks confused. 'Wiped? Phone?'

Beside me, Tri murmurs quietly, 'She's from the nineteenth century.'

'Enough of all this,' Missy is saying. 'We shall continue tomorrow.'

'Actually, Jamie's right.' Tri speaks more firmly. 'This building is probably going to be demolished.'

TRI

It's as if something snaps* within her.

As the words leave my lips, the ghost called Missy turns to the piano and thumps the keyboard again and again, with both arms.

She begins to fade*. Soon nothing can be seen and slowly the noise becomes more distant* until we are alone in a silent music room.

That went well,' says Jamie.

Chapter 10

JAMIE

The trouble starts immediately.

As I approach school the next morning, I hear the fire alarm.

I walk through the school gates and see that all the children who have arrived have been gathered at the far end of the playground.

Teachers are running around like crazy chickens.

What's going on?

Moments later, I hear the loud, jangling bells of fire* engines approaching. Two of them pull up outside the gate behind me and three firemen jump out and run into the school

TRI

I am a bit late that morning. When I arrive, the fire engines are just driving off.

We are all going into school when there is a loud ringing in the hall.

'Don't worry, it's just the burglar* alarm now.' Mr Attiah is standing at the door of his office. 'It never rains but it pours.'

After a few seconds, the alarm stops. Then, at the same time, everyone's mobile phones start ringing.

Things are getting seriously weird.

MARKO

I know what is happening.

As soon as I hear the alarm, I understand.

JAMIE

We're laughing and chatting in our classroom when Miss Phelps walks in, trying to act as if nothing unusual has happened.

Phelpsy tells us that in today's Geography lesson, we are going to learn about volcanoes. She switches* on the laptop on her desk to project a picture on to the screen at the front of the class.

Nothing happens. The screen stays empty.

MARKO

In my class, Miss Gordon is meant to be starting the lesson but she can't stop looking at her mobile phone.

Miss Gordon: 'All right. Who's been playing with my phone? It was working when I arrived this morning.'

The door opens. It's Mr Attiah.

Mr Attiah: 'Miss Gordon, I'm afraid the school computer system appears* to be down.'

Miss Gordon: 'Like my phone.'

Mr Attiah frowns and takes his phone from his pocket.

He looks at it, then swipes the screen. Then taps it.

Mr Attiah: 'What's going on?'

I'm at the back of the class with one thought in my head.

It's Missy.

And she's really angry.

TRI

Break comes early, and for one simple reason: the school is falling apart.

All morning alarms go off, then stop, phones start ringing, the dinner bell sounds for no reason.

Mr Attiah switches off the electricity* supply. That's when someone discovers all the books in the library have been pulled off their shelves. When the school orchestra gathers for a rehearsal* in the school hall, all the instruments are out of tune.

I find Jamie and Marko together in the playground, staring through the window of the Old Music Room.

MARKO

ME: 'She's not there anymore. She's moved into the school.'

JAMIE: 'We should tell someone.'

TRI: 'Oh yeah, right. What do we say? "Excuse me, Mr Attiah, but we happen to know that the ghost of a music teacher who died over a century ago is haunting* the school"?'

JAMIE: 'Maybe she'll get bored.'

TRI: 'I don't know much about ghosts, but I'm guessing that, if you've been hanging around for 150 years, boredom isn't exactly an issue.'

JAMIE

There's not much teaching that day. Men in overalls go into classrooms. They look at the electricity connections* and study the computers.

As soon as the power comes back on, the alarms start again.

At the end of the day, each of us is given a sealed letter. We are told not to open it ourselves but to give it to our parents.

As soon as I'm out of the gates, I open it.

TRI

Jamie shows me the letter. We read it together.

Barrow Hill High School

George Attiah

Headmaster

Dear Parents

We regret having to tell you that events have occurred* at our school today over which we have no control.

There have been major problems with the electricity supply which we believe has affected* computers, musical instruments and has possibly even caused books to fall off shelves.

We are concerned* above all for the safety of the children. For this reason, we have decided to close the school for the rest of the week.

We shall keep you informed. In the meantime, please accept our apologies for this inconvenience*.

Yours

George Attiah

Chapter 11

TRI

I can't sleep that night. All I can think about is Missy. I feel bad about causing all the trouble by telling her that the Old Music Room is going to be demolished.

Some time in the early hours of the morning, I get up, reach for my school bag, which I have left on my desk, and reach into it for the book I'm reading at the moment.

My hand touches something unfamiliar*. It feels like a leather book, but it's strangely cold, as if it has been left in a fridge.

Slowly, I take it out.

I am holding a small, battered old leather notebook. Written on the cover, in neat handwriting and faded ink, are the words:

THE PRIVATE DIARY OF MISS DOROTHEA BRYANT

For some reason, I look around me. It's Missy's diary. How on earth did it end up in my bag? And who put it there?

I take the diary back to bed. I carefully open it, and start to read.

Monday, April 3rd 1881

Arose at 6, breakfast at 7. I confess* that am not able to eat much, such is my excitement. Today is my first day as a teacher at Barrow Hill School. My dream of being a teacher is about to come true.

At the school, I find the teachers to be polite, if a little cold. The headmaster, Mr Theobald, has a fierce look to him, but there is, I think, a twinkle of humour in his eyes!

He introduces me to my class, most of whom seem too nervous to speak. Mr Theobald has been teaching them hymns.

I hope to offer some more cheerful tunes to the children in the future, but will keep this information to myself for the moment.

The next few pages of the diary describe Miss Bryant's first term* at school. She gets the children to call her 'Missy'. When one of the boys tells her that his father has forbidden him to play the piano on the grounds that it is for women and girls, she tells him music is for everyone.

Quite soon, she runs into trouble.

Wednesday, June 22nd 1881

An unpleasant scene with Miss Billington (History and Religious Studies). Every time she sees me, she criticises me for wearing my hair loose*. According to Miss B, my `wild hairstyle´ is `unsuitable* for a teacher´.

Well! I am quite firm on the matter, telling her that I do not tie my hair back because I find it uncomfortable.

Her reply is that `ladies should expect discomfort´. As she speaks, her eyes are not on my hair, but on my waist*. I fear that she has noticed that I prefer not to wear a corset to work.´

As I read, I begin to think that Missy is an odd mixture of innocent* and intelligent. She tells her girls that they should have careers* because 'women are not cattle*, born only to reproduce*, but humans'. I'm cheering for her, but I'm worried for her, too.

It's late and I feel tired. There will be more time to read the diary in the morning. Before I put it aside*, I read the last entry, dated September 2nd 1883. It's the day before the fire.

I am feeling so miserable that I find it difficult to write down the events of this sorry day.

On arrival at school this morning, I was called to the office of the headmaster. There, waiting for me with a serious look on their faces, were Mr Theobald, Miss Billington and the school vicar*, the Reverend Jameson-Smythe.

The headmaster read me a letter he received from a group of parents. They accused* me of wearing my hair in a way that was `not ladylike´ and of introducing the ungodly tunes of the music hall into the classroom. I am also accused of `putting dangerous ideas´ into the minds of my young pupils.

After the letter had been read, Miss Billington told me that what she calls my `dangerous, free-thinking nonsense´ had no place in a God-fearing school. The vicar stood by, a look of silent distaste on his face.

There is nothing more to say. I have to leave the school at the end of this week. Today is a truly sad and terrible day for me.

I switch off the light, my thoughts full of Missy, and soon fall asleep.

I awake early and reach for the diary.

It's gone.

Chapter 12

JAMIE

My parents think they know me.

They're wrong.

Because I don't scream and shout after they tell me that they are taking me away from Barrow Hill School to bright, shiny, brilliant St Matthews, they think that means I'm OK with it.

Wrong again, guys.

I'm planning.

On the day when a ghost has given us a day off school, Lisbeth wakes me up by coming into my bedroom and using me as a trampoline. Then my mother is there, drawing the curtains* and giving a long, bossy lecture* about how I mustn't stay in bed all day.

They leave. The house is silent.

I'm in bed. I wonder to myself whether my parents would change their minds if Barrow Hill School were moved somewhere else.

No way.

And what would happen if I got a brilliant end-of-term report and promised never to talk to Tri or Marko again?

Nothing. My mother is proud of never changing her mind. Her favourite sentence is, 'When I say something, I mean it.'

I lie in my bed, dreaming of a life of freedom.

I'll just go, run away. I've got enough money saved for a train ticket. I'll take a rucksack and my guitar. I'll earn money by playing on street corners. Maybe I'll get discovered and appear* on a TV talent show.

That will be the next time my parents will see their son – famous and on TV.

'Yes!' I laugh out loud at the thought.

'No.'

What's that? I sit up in bed. Am I dreaming? Then it's there again, all around me, filling the room.

'No, Jamie.'

I lie back in bed. I thought I was alone but I'm not.

Missy is here and, of course, she's right. Running away is not the answer.

Another plan occurs to me that afternoon when I am walking down the High Street, thinking about what my mother said when she told me about St Matthews.

She told me I needed to 'keep my nose clean' for the rest of term.

There's a reason for that. St Matthews is bright, shiny and brilliant for a reason: you have to be almost perfect to get in. They'd love Tri, for example, but they wouldn't even look at Marko.

What if I *don't* keep my nose clean? What would happen if I got so dirty that only one school in the area would take me?

Barrow Hill.

At this point, I remember the matches I found in the park and my brilliant, dangerous idea:

Jamie, the crazy little fire starter.

It's perfect.

Across the street, as if life has read my mind,
I see a petrol* station.

I walk towards it, walk into the shop by the petrol
pumps. By the till, there are plastic canisters.
I take two, then walk outside to fill them with
petrol.

When I walk in to pay, the lady behind the till
glances at me suspiciously. She knows I'm too
young to buy petrol.

I give her the look. She shrugs, then takes the
money.

It's good being bad.

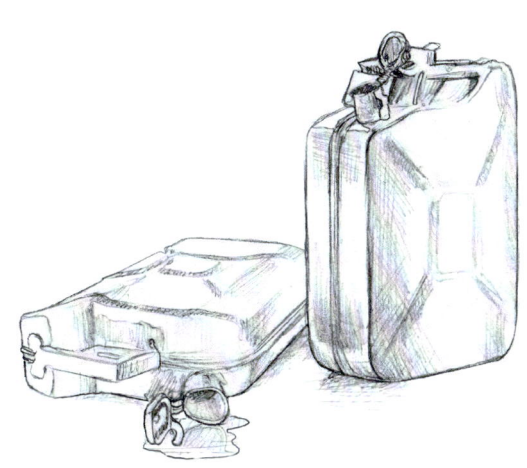

Chapter 13

MARKO

It's a bad, bad day.

I can't escape to school. I'm trapped* at home with my nan.

And her bottle.

She reads the letter from Mr Attiah at breakfast.

NAN: 'Oh no. This does my head* in. What does it mean?'

Everything does my nan's head in.

ME: 'It just means I have to stay at home today.'

NAN: 'Oh all right, you can help me do the housework.'

ME: 'All right, then.'

After breakfast, she tells me she's going to start the housework by clearing out the kitchen cupboard.

In the cupboard, she finds her best friend.

NAN: 'Oh look. What a piece of luck.'

She takes out the bottle and pours the first drink of the day.

It's going to be a long day.

I stay with her as she watches TV.

One rubbish programme follows another.

Every minute feels like an hour.

I miss my mum.

That night I have the strangest dream.

It's very dark. I am walking down a street in a town I have never seen before.

Someone is holding my hand. I look up. It's Missy.

Her eyes are bright and shiny. A smile is on her face, as if she has a really great secret that she can't wait to tell.

People are coming out of pubs but the sight of a woman in a Victorian dress walking down the streets holding the hand of a child in his pyjamas doesn't seem to bother* them at all. They just smile at us.

Together, we walk down a narrow street. It leads into a field.

In the shadows, I see the shapes of carousels and swings*. We're walking through a fairground*, but it's dark and all the rides have closed.

On the edge of the field, there are four caravans*. Missy walks to the smallest caravan, then stops.

MISSY: 'Go in, Marko. She's waiting for you.'

She?

In my dream I feel confused and scared.

I walk up the steps. I open the door to the caravan.

It's dark inside. On the far side, I can hear the sound of someone sleeping.

Just from the sound of the breath, I know who that person is.

ME: 'Mum?'

She turns over immediately. It's almost as if she has been expecting me.

MUM: 'Marko?'

I say nothing.

MUM: 'Marko, is that you?'

ME: 'Come home, Mum.'

MUM: 'How did you get here?'

ME: 'Come home.'

She opens her arms to me. I walk forwards. I bury* my face into her shoulder. It feels soft.

I open my eyes. I wake from my dream.

I'm holding my pillow.

Chapter 14

JAMIE

It turns out we were wrong about Missy and her big ghostly nervous* breakdown. On the day that the school is closed, she begins to calm down. The alarms no longer go off without warning. Someone switches on a computer and it works.

I talk to Tri about this at lunch-time on the day we return to school.

'I think she's gone,' Tri says. 'She's made her point and now she's going to leave the school alone.'

I remember the voice I heard yesterday, the voice which stopped me running away from home.

'No,' I say quietly. 'She's still here.'

TRI

That afternoon, Miss Phelps surprises us.

She's quite nice. She tells us she was impressed by how calm we stayed during what she calls 'our

little electrical problems'. Now life can get back to normal.

I put up my hand. 'How can we get back to normal when the music room is locked and we can't practise for the Christmas concert?'

'You can practise in the assembly hall, Katrina. There's a piano there.'

Jamie puts up a hand. 'What about Eye Trouble, Miss Phelps?'

Miss Phelps is still smiling at me. She ignores Jamie.

'You're playing solo, aren't you, Katrina?'

Before I can reply, she has turned away.

'I think you should,' she says, ending the conversation. 'You're very good solo.'

With her back turned, she laughs and mutters something, just loud enough for the class to hear.

'Eye Trouble. How ridiculous* is that?'

MARKO

Tri comes looking for me after the last lesson of the day. She seems a bit upset.

TRI: 'We're having a band practice in the assembly hall. They want me to play solo but I don't care. Are you coming?'

ME: 'I'll be there in five minutes. But –'

And she's gone.

JAMIE

Tri is at the piano in the assembly hall. Her conversation with Miss Phelps this afternoon seems to have upset her big-time.

'We need a song that involves* the whole band.' She plays a few chords* on the piano.

'I've written a song about Missy,' she calls out over the music.

She starts singing.

TRI

She was a music teacher

In their little school

They told her to teach by rote*

All the right notes

Teach the kids to obey* the rules.

But she sang her own sweet song

And it's the song of history

Told the girls and boys

To make some noise

If they wanted to be free.

JAMIE

It's a good tune and it's got a catchy beat. It's got attitude*.

'But it needs something else, right?' As usual, Tri reads my mind. 'A different rhythm. Maybe a change of key*?'

As if by magic, I hear a slow, old-fashioned melody in my head. Now where did that come from?

I turn to Marko.

'That song Missy was playing,' I say. 'How did it go?'

Marko switches on his bass amp*, then closes his eyes, as if he is listening to something very, very carefully.

MARKO

I hear her voice in my head.

> *Every night when the sun goes down,*
>
> *Every night when the sun goes down,*
>
> *Every night when the sun goes down,*
>
> *I hang my head and cry.'*

Tri and Jamie are staring at me.

ME: 'That was the song Missy was singing.'

Tri: 'It doesn't really fit with what I was playing, though.'

Jamie: 'Wait.'

He picks up his guitar and plays the chords Tri was playing. Then he changes key, slows the tempo. He looks up and smiles.

Jamie: 'And from there we go into Missy's song. Is there a second verse?'

TRI

This is where things become a little bit weird.

As Marko plays the bass, the keys on the piano start to move. They are being played by invisible* hands.

MARKO

I wish every day that I could go home,

I wish every day that I could go home,

I wish every day that I could go home,

I hang my head and cry.

JAMIE

Tri does the verse, Marko sings the slow chorus and I do the linking guitar.

'Missy's here,' says Marko at one point. 'She's helping us.'

Tri looks at me and I shrug.

Ghost power?

Maybe. Maybe not.

Either way, we've got our song.

Chapter 15

TRI

Here's how the Christmas concert works.

For the first part of the evening, the younger classes perform. There's a choir, some poetry, a few solo acts. In the second half, some teachers play some ancient* pop songs to warm up the audience. Everyone likes to see teachers letting their hair down (even if they've got no hair to let down).

Then the two top years get to show off. They are always the stars of the show.

Not tonight though.

We are the last act of the first half.

And we are going to smash it.

JAMIE

The assembly hall is full of mums, dads, brothers and sisters. Everyone is there, except (surprise, surprise) my parents. They have told me that,

since I will be leaving the school, it would be 'inappropriate'*.

Maybe they think that no one will notice their son anyway.

Tonight they are about as wrong as they could ever be.

MARKO

Something big is coming.

I think it's going to be good, but I'm not completely sure.

I feel Missy beside me.

She makes me strong.

TRI

During the first half, we watch from backstage. I notice that Jamie is in one of his strange moods. His face is pale and there's a distant look in his eyes and I worry that he's not thinking about the concert.

By the time we are due* to go on stage, the audience is restless*. There's chatting in the hall as Miss Phelps introduces us.

'And now,' she says in the friendly voice she puts on for parents,' we have Year Eight's own pop group. It's Me Trouble!'

Jamie groans*, but there's no time even to be annoyed* that she has got our name wrong.

We're on.

JAMIE

At first it goes to plan.

We take up our positions, plug in, check the tuning. We've decided to start with the slow melody, sung by Marko, before Tri kicks in with her verse.

She plays the verse through, then pauses for Marko to start singing.

He doesn't. He's staring down at the front row*.

Everyone in the hall is waiting.

He breaks the silence with one word.

MARKO

ME: 'Mum!'

TRI

There are some nervous laughs in the hall, but most of the audience think it's part of the performance.

I decide to play the melody through again. As the notes reach him, Marko slowly looks up. I begin to breathe again.

He's back.

Every night when the sun goes down…

JAMIE

When Marko starts singing, there's a sort* of gasp in the hall.

He was good at rehearsal, but on stage he is a different person. He is a natural performer.

Every note he sings tells the story of pain* and sadness that only he can know and only this song can tell.

I play some guitar and Tri comes in. The audience start clapping in time. Then we slow down, and it's time for Marko again.

*I've wished every day that you
would come home…*

He's looking down to the front row. There's a pretty red-haired woman staring at him. Tears are running down her cheeks*.

*I've wished every day that you
would come home…*

He has changed the words but it doesn't matter. Nothing matters now.

I hang my head and cry.

MARKO

I finish.

There is a roar in front of me. People are standing up, shouting and stamping their feet.

I only see one person.

TRI

As soon as we are backstage for the interval*, Marko disappears* to find his mum.

I sense* that Jamie is feeling disappointed that no one from his family is there.

'Come and see my parents,' I say. 'My dad will want to talk to you about how you put that song together.'

Jamie looks at me, an odd smile on his face.

'I'll catch you in a minute,' he says. 'I've just got to do something first.'

Five minutes later, I am in the hall, surrounded* by people talking about the song, when I hear a voice within me.

Jamie!

At first, I think it must be tiredness or excitement. Then I hear it again.

Jamie. Save Jamie.

I run for the door.

Chapter 16

JAMIE

It's dark. Peaceful.

In my head, the sound of the audience fades. In my nose is the smell of petrol*.

There is not much room inside the shed*, but now I am ready. I have brought in the two cans I had hidden in a rubbish bin* near the school gate.

I open one and splash some petrol around me.

My plan is to get the fire going, let myself out, then watch from the playground.

Simple.

I strike* a match*. It flares* up and catches my finger. I drop it.

There's a sudden roar, and suddenly flames are all around me.

I grab for the handle* and pull.

It comes away in my hand.

TRI

I'm standing on the school steps, looking across the playground, when I hear a strange, muffled sound.

Then silence.

There's a smell in the air.

Smoke.

JAMIE

The shed has no windows. I beat against the door once, then twice.

The smoke is in my lungs*. I try to scream but I can't make a sound.

And that's the last thing I remember.

TRI

As soon as I see smoke coming from the shed beside the Old Music Room, I am running across the playground, yelling for help.

When I reach the shed, I can hear the crackle* of burning from inside.

I reach for the door handle but it has fallen off. I push against the door. It's jammed.

'Missy!' I scream. 'Help us!'

MARKO

It's like a kick in the stomach.

ME: 'Something's wrong.'

MUM: 'Nothing's wrong, love. I'm home now. You're all right.'

ME: 'No!'

I sprint across the hall, pushing parents and teachers out of the way.

TRI

Suddenly Marko's beside me.

'Take a run at it,' he shouts.

He pulls me back 10 feet from the shed door.

'Together!' he shouts. 'One, two, go!'

MARKO

My dad once showed me how to break through a locked door.

Kick it near the lock with all your strength*.

We reach the door. I fly through the air, feet first. I kick both legs with all my strength.

There is a loud crack of wood.

There's smoke everywhere.

TRI

The flames roar ahead of us, burning our faces.

I drop to my knees and feel around. I touch something.

'Jamie!'

Together, Marko and I pull Jamie's unconscious* body out of the blazing* shed.

MARKO

Parents are all around us. People are shouting.

Someone crouches over Jamie.

ONE OF THE MUMS: 'He's breathing. Stand back.'

Jamie opens his eyes.

JAMIE

The skin on my face and hands hurts and my throat* burns. My back was scraped* when they pulled me out of the shed.

But I'm all right.

I walk between Tri and Marko towards the Old Music Room. Someone has unlocked the door.

With a groan, I lie down gently on the floor.

TRI

There's some serious teacher panic going on. Parts of the muttered conversation from adults standing at the door reach us as we sit on the floor beside Jamie.

'An ambulance has been called.'

'His parents are on their way.'

'So lucky.'

'A miracle.'

I look at Jamie, then at Marko.

We smile.

MARKO

It feels like no one else is there.

Just the three of us.

No.

Four.

JAMIE

Lying there, I look across the Old Music Room. Someone, it seems to me, is sitting at the piano.

As if from far away, I hear music.

And then she's there.

TRI

Missy.

We can see her, swaying backwards and forwards as she plays, her hair as wild as ever.

I glance at the adults. They are talking among themselves. It's as if we are in another world.

JAMIE

And, as we watch Missy, the strangest thing happens.

She helps us to see, in those seconds, what the future holds for each of us.

MARKO

People are going to talk about my singing.

Teachers are going to be different towards me.

Bullies will pretend they were always my friend.

And Mum will be back.

She will be back to stay.

It's going to be all right.

JAMIE

There will be trouble, of course. My parents will talk to the school.

At the end of it all, they will reach a surprising decision. After she has spoken to Mr Attiah, my mother will break the rule of a lifetime – she will change her mind. I will stay at Barrow Hill.

There will be an article in the local paper about how a band called Eye Trouble took an old song and a new song and created something unusual. We'll get asked to play at parties. In conversations about me, I will hear a new word.

Talent.

TRI

I watch her as she plays, and suddenly I understand.

Saving Jamie, like she saved the three children all those years ago, has set Missy free.

After today, she will go to wherever ghosts live when they no longer have to wander on earth. She will go home.

And yet – she will always be with us.

She will be watching me as I make music, when I am practising, when I am performing.

Each of us – Jamie, Marko and me – will know that she's there.

Through the good times and bad times, we shall hear the song of Miss Dorothea Bryant.

Every night when the sun goes down…

And we'll remember the ghost who changed our lives.

1. Auflage 7 | 2025

Alle Drucke dieser Auflage sind unverändert und können im Unterricht nebeneinander verwendet werden.
Die letzte Zahl bezeichnet das Jahr des Druckes. Das Werk und seine Teile sind urheberrechtlich geschützt. Jede Nutzung in anderen als den gesetzlich zugelassenen Fällen bedarf der vorherigen schriftlichen Einwilligung des Verlages.

Autor: Terence Blacker
Redaktion: Don Haupt
Layoutkonzeption: Maja Merz
Illustrationen: Claudia Flor
Gestaltung und Satz: Joachim Schrimm, bostext, Friolzheim
Umschlaggestaltung: Maja Merz
Titelbild: Claudia Flor
Tonregie und Schnitt: JMS Group Limited, Hethersett, Norwich
Sprecher: Terence Blacker

Druck und Bindung: Plump Druck & Medien GmbH, Rheinbreitbach

Printed in Germany
ISBN 978-3-12-530906-7